'This is a [illegible] *tten. Paul is a fine Bible* [illegible] *and this book carries a po*[illegible]*ok it to heart, I think that Satan's work would suffer a serious setback!'*

Bishop Wallace Benn

'This is an excellent and much-needed book. It is not only highly "readable" but also penetrating in its analysis of the Bible's teaching on the wretched sin of gossip. Readers will find it both challenging and encouraging. May it be used by God to bring about greater godliness among his people. I recommend it wholeheartedly.'

William Taylor, Rector, St Helen's Bishopsgate

'This little book packs a powerful punch. It is the Bible book of Proverbs taught prophetically. By that I mean it's a clear word from the Lord to us right now and to his church, declaring the problem, convicting of sin and calling for repentance, faith and renewal by the Holy Spirit. It's filled with pastoral insights and a winsome call to be like our wonderful Lord Jesus Christ.'

Bishop Tim Davies

JUST BETWEEN YOU AND ME

JUST BETWEEN YOU AND ME

A SEARCHING LOOK AT THE SERIOUS PROBLEM OF GOSSIP

PAUL WILLIAMS

PAW

First published in Great Britain in 2025

British Library Cataloguing in Publication Data
A record for this book is available from the British Library

ISBN: 978-1-0683593-0-9

Designed by Pete Barnsley (CreativeHoot.com)

Printed in the UK

Dedicated to all those who
have been affected by the
destructive sin of gossip.

CONTENTS

A WORD OF THANKS

With every book I've written there have been others behind me and alongside me, encouraging me and advising me. This book is no exception to that, but more than any other of my writings, it would never have been published without the support and encouragement of a bunch of people. So while I take responsibility for the content, if this book is helpful at all, then it is thanks to the following people. William, Wes and the Great St Helen's Trust trustees created the space for me to write. Julia read the first draft, gave me excellent feedback and urged me to keep going. Pete, Tom, Bob, David and David spent countless hours keeping me afloat. Leo and Chevonne helped me believe it was a worthwhile work. Not least of all, James was incredibly supportive after reading an initial draft and then not only urged me but also enabled me to get this book to print. Thank you to you all and to others who have given me words of encouragement along the way.

Thanks also to my incredible family, who remain rock solid in their support of me: Caroline, Susannah, Bethan and Dan, Joshua, and Elle. I love you and am thankful every day for your love for me.

INTRODUCTION:

THE CONFESSION I'VE NEVER HEARD

In the past 30 years of my Christian ministry, people have walked into my study and confessed many different things. In floods of tears desperate people have told me that they've committed adultery, become addicted to hard porn or been cross-dressing for years. Others have hung their head in shame as they've admitted to lying, to substance abuse and to embezzling company funds. I've had people wanting to unburden themselves as they've sought help with problems arising from anger and pride and selfish ambition. Over many years, many people have confessed many things to me.

That said, there are a number of sins I have *never* had to deal with pastorally. No-one has ever confessed to murder and no-one has ever disclosed any type of incestuous relationship. That might not surprise you, but what does surprise me – and I think it should surprise you too – is that no-one has ever walked into my study to confess the sin of gossip. The reason this is surprising is because, sadly, gossip is a widespread problem in the church and a persistent sin in the lives of many Christians. And gossip is no small thing. Gossip causes considerable pain. I know people who have been seriously hurt by gossip. Some have been utterly broken and ruined by it. And I'm thinking of Christians here, who have been gossiped about by other *Christians*.

Gossip is a very destructive sin, and as such it is roundly condemned in the Bible. Just look at Romans 1:29–31 and note the dubious company that gossip keeps:

> They have become filled with every kind of wickedness, evil, greed and depravity. They are full of envy, murder, strife, deceit and malice. They are *gossips*, slanderers, God-haters, insolent, arrogant and boastful; they invent ways of doing evil; they disobey their parents; they have no understanding, no fidelity, no love, no mercy (emphasis mine).

In this devastating list of wickedness, those who gossip are put alongside God-haters and murderers! As far as the Bible is concerned, gossip is a very serious problem. If that's a surprise to you, then the very next verse might rock you to your boots, for Romans 1:32 says that doing things such as gossiping deserve death:

> Although they know God's righteous decree that those who do such things deserve death, they not only continue to do these very things but also approve of those who practice them.

This section of Romans 1 paints a vivid picture of a godless society – a society under the wrath of God. It tells us that a culture that has turned its back on God will not only be characterised by these wicked things but will even approve of those who practise them. Sound familiar? Of course it does. It's the world we live in. In 21st-century Britain many of the sins listed in Romans 1 are actually approved of – including gossip. So we find gossip columns in our daily newspapers. And I'm not just thinking about the newspapers that used to be described, rather pejoratively by some, as 'the tabloids'. Even *The Times* and the BBC Sports app have a gossip column! Our society's approval of gossip identifies us, according to Romans, as a godless society.

But, desperately, it's not just 'out there' in the world that gossip flourishes. Sadly, gossip is alive and kicking in the church too.

Gossip is a serious problem for far too many committed Christian people. That is why it is so surprising that, over three decades of pastoral ministry, not one person has ever confessed to me the sin of gossip or asked for help to overcome it.

I wonder if the reason is because, largely, we don't see it as a particularly serious problem. To use the title of another book, it is considered a 'respectable sin'.[1] It seems that gossip is acceptable in many (dare I suggest 'most'?) Christian circles. Let me clarify what I mean. I don't for one minute think that any mature Christian would try to argue that there's a time or a place when gossip is acceptable. However, we do seem ready to live with gossip and treat it as something that doesn't need to be challenged. To make my point, let me ask you how often have you heard the sin of gossip raised in a sermon or Bible study?

Gossip is one of the sins the apostle Paul is worried he'll encounter when he arrives in Corinth. At the time he wrote 2 Corinthians, the church in Corinth was being led astray by false teachers and Paul was trying to persuade the church to return to apostolic Christianity. Paul fears that when he visits the Corinthians, he'll discover a number of ugly things in the church including gossip:

> For I am afraid that when I come I may not find you as I want you to be, and you may not find me as you want me to be. I fear that there may be discord, jealousy, fits of rage, selfish ambition, slander, *gossip*, arrogance and disorder (2 Corinthians 12:20, emphasis mine).

It's another devastating list of sins – a list that is symptomatic of deep and serious problems in the church – and gossip sits squarely in the middle.

So it's an oversight that we rarely address the problem of gossip because it's *one* mark of a church that's not in great shape. And it's so damaging – as anyone who's been on the receiving end of gossip will be all too painfully aware. It ruins relationships. It demolishes lives. It trashes reputations. Gossip has ended careers, wrecked marriages and defamed characters. Gossip can even lead to death. Just think of times when malicious journalism and social media frenzies have spread and fuelled rumours about celebrities, causing them such mental distress that the celebrity in question has been driven to take their own life. Gossip kills. For something that is so destructive, I will never understand why we don't feel the need to preach against it, confess it, repent of it and at least try to eradicate it from our fellowships.

This little book is an attempt to address the problem. It's a study of what the Bible says about gossip, most of which is found in the book of Proverbs. It's written for everyone, because every one of us is tempted to gossip. It's written for those who've been hurt by gossip.

My prayer is that many people who read this book will face up to the fact that gossip is a problem in their lives – and, as a result, will want to repent of their gossiping and take steps to weed it out.

My prayer is that these pages will change the culture in our churches by helping us see how devastating, destructive and damaging gossip is.

My prayer is that we would come to hate gossip. I long that we would abhor gossip to the point where we can't bear the thought of even the slightest gossipy comment leaving our lips – and we certainly don't want to listen to it.

My prayer is that we'd not tolerate gossip in our church communities because we know how dangerous it is.

The question is: if gossip is really as bad as I suggest, why do we do it?

1 GOSSIP IS TASTY

I love chocolate. I love every kind of chocolate – plain chocolate, white chocolate, dark chocolate. I love chocolate in any form – in a box, in a bar or in a fountain! I love chocolate so much that when there's some in the house, I have to muster up all the self-control available to man if I'm to refrain from eating it. And I dare not eat too much of that delicious, calorie-rich confectionary because otherwise I quickly pile on the pounds!

In the light of this revelation, you won't be surprised to hear that, when dining out, I'll choose a chocolate option on the dessert menu every time. My wife, Caroline, on the other hand, prefers savoury food. For her, an appetising starter is the icing on the cake of a good meal (if you'll excuse that rather bamboozling mixed metaphor!).

Now whether you're a sweet or savoury person – and whether you most enjoy a starter, a main course or, like me, a sumptuous chocolaty dessert – you'll know the satisfying delight of eating and savouring delicious food. The moment I take the first mouthful of a 'death by chocolate' pudding, my taste buds send my neurotransmitters and brain receptors into overdrive, releasing dopamine which makes me feel good – very, very good. That's what makes chocolate so addictive.

Here's the point of all this talk about eating delicious food: we can get that same feel-good factor when we consume the words of a gossip. Gossip 'tastes' delicious, and as a result, we find it very hard to resist.

The book of Proverbs tells us:

> The words of a gossip are like choice morsels
> *(Proverbs 18:8 and 26:22).*

Choice morsels are portions of the best and most scrumptious food. An earful of gossip is like a mouthful of the most delectable food, because it gives us a delicious tingle inside. So if we're out with friends and find the words of a gossip on the menu, the temptation to gobble them up is very strong.

Proverbs 18:8 warns us that gossip always goes down a treat – whether we start with gossip, or whether it's the main course of our discussion, or whether gossip is the dessert that rounds off the evening.

But allow me to stop here for a minute. With Proverbs 18:8 before us, those with a tender conscience could be feeling very guilty of listening to gossip, even when they've done no such thing. On the other hand, because we are so good at justifying our actions, others of us will find it very easy to excuse our gossipy actions as nothing more than sharing important information. Jeremiah wrote that the 'heart is deceitful above all things' (Jeremiah 17:9). Since we are so devious, and are prone to deceive even ourselves, it's important that we have a clear understanding of what is and isn't gossip.

Let's be clear that there are situations when important and sensitive information needs to be shared. For example, when interviewing someone for a job, it's important that the interview panel is fully informed of things disclosed by a candidate or their referees. Sharing information in that setting is not gossip.

The same is true at a personal level. We need support and wisdom from others, so at times we need to be able to unload and share things with people confidentially.

Healthy churches will cultivate a culture of deep meaningful relationships where we support one another and pray for each other intelligently.

Sharing information with someone appropriately is not gossip. But – and this is a big but – we know that people share information under the guise of it being for prayer or support when their motive is actually to spread incriminating information.

The *Cambridge Dictionary* defines gossip as: 'Casual or unconstrained conversation or reports about other people, typically involving details that are not confirmed as being true.' Sharing untruths is a good start towards defining gossip, but it's quite possible to be gossiping about things that *are* true but shouldn't be shared. For example, we might say things that are true but with a desire to hurt someone.

I am told that the Hebrew term translated as 'a gossip' describes someone who reveals secrets. It's the idea of someone who tells tales, spreads scandal and starts rumour. One website gives this helpful definition: 'A gossiper is a person who has privileged information about people and proceeds to reveal that information to those who have no business knowing it.'[1] The same website helpfully suggests two ways that gossip is different from legitimately or appropriately sharing information.

The first is intent. We are guilty of gossip when we share information in order either to make others look bad or to make ourselves look good. We might also tell people information in order to promote ourselves as someone who's very important simply by being in possession of information.

The second way concerns the type of information we share:

> Gossipers speak of the faults and failings of others, or reveal potentially embarrassing or shameful details regarding the lives of others, without their knowledge or approval. Even if they mean no harm, it is still gossip.

The first part of this definition is probably what we most obviously think of as gossip: intentionally speaking badly of others. But note the phrase towards the end of that definition – 'even if the teller meant no harm'. This is very important. Even if it might not be our intention to cause someone harm, when we pass on information that was shared with us in confidence, we have gossiped. Simply having a loose tongue and thoughtlessly letting something slip should be considered gossip.

As we go through this book, then, I am working on the premise that gossip is about both the intent or motive for sharing information, as well as the type of information we share. It's crucial we take this seriously, because it's very easy to convince ourselves that we're not gossips. Who wants that label attached to them?

Being honest with ourselves and being clear about what counts as gossip is vital, because we are fallen human beings. To return to the opening words from Proverbs, gossip is 'like choice morsels' – it tastes delicious to us; we love consuming it; we find it very hard to resist. But resist it we must, because gossip is immensely destructive.

2
GOSSIP DESTROYS

I vividly remember watching the bombing of Iraq at the beginning of the Gulf War as real-time images were shown live on TV. As I saw missiles raining down on Baghdad and demolishing building after building, it broke my heart to think of the catastrophic loss of life. I sat in front of the television with tears streaming down my face as the city was destroyed. The destruction of a city is devastating, but it's not only cruise missiles that can destroy a city – gossip can too.

> Through the blessing of the upright a city is exalted,
> but by the mouth of the wicked it is destroyed.
> *(Proverbs 11:11)*

At first reading this proverb could be dismissed as hyperbole. It appears to read like an over-sensationalised newspaper headline. A city destroyed by words – really?

But before you write this off as an overstatement of epic proportions, know that history has shown that unverified but plausible-sounding gossip has been the basis for death and destruction on a gargantuan scale.

Here's one example I found on the internet:

> In the 14th century, thousands of Jews were killed in response to rumours that Satan was protecting them from the plague in exchange for poisoning the wells of Christians. In 1321 in Guienne, France alone, an estimated 5000 Jews were burned alive for supposedly poisoning wells.[1]

The mouth of the wicked destroys.

More recently, Vladimir Putin has justified the war in Ukraine by speaking false accusations. Putin's propaganda machine has attempted to persuade the Russian public that his 'military operation' was launched in order to protect neighbouring Ukrainian citizens from the policies of their government, which Russian propaganda labelled as a 'neo-Nazi regime'. Putin denounced alleged 'genocide' carried out by Kyiv in the Ukrainian separatist territories of Donetsk and Lugansk, portraying Kyiv as the worst of villains. This malicious gossip has been the justification for the most deplorable destruction.

Words are very powerful:

> The tongue has the power of life and death,
> 	and those who love it will eat its fruit.
>
> *(Proverbs 18:21)*

Words *can* be used for great good. With well-chosen words a skilled negotiator can transform tense and dangerous situations. A gifted arbitrator can bring two seemingly entrenched opponents to an agreement where both can walk away with no loss of reputation. Encouraging words can transform someone who is dejected and defeated into a positive person who believes they can overcome. Words have 'the power of life'. But words can also tear down. They have 'the power of … death'. Gossip is one way that words can be used to destroy. Words can create suspicion. Words can destroy a city. Churches too can be wrecked by gossip. Gossip destroys.

The book of Proverbs tells us that:

1. Words of gossip destroy friendship

…a gossip separates close friends.
(Proverbs 16:28)

2. Words of gossip destroy trust

A gossip betrays a confidence;
so avoid anyone who talks too much.
(Proverbs 20:19)

3. Words of gossip destroy peace – causing conflict

A perverse person stirs up conflict…
(Proverbs 16:28)

Gossip is destructive. Do not underestimate the power of words to destroy whole cities. And do not underestimate the destructive impact that gossip can have on individuals and whole communities, because gossip is poisonous.

3

GOSSIP IS POISONOUS

I love rhubarb. Rhubarb is the wonderfully sharp, mouth-puckering taste that makes many classic British dishes. I especially enjoy it when combined with something sweet. If you've never been that taken with rhubarb, try it in a crumble or with custard – or better still, in a crumble with custard. Rhubarb is delicious.

If I'm giving you the urge to cook some of those delicious sticks of gorgeousness, and if you've never prepared rhubarb before, I need to warn you: DO NOT COOK THE LEAVES! Please be sure to heed that warning because the leaves of the rhubarb plant are deadly. They contain oxalic acid, which causes burning in the mouth and throat, breathing difficulties, coma and even death. Admittedly, you would have to consume a huge quantity of rhubarb leaves for them to kill you – around 5kg I'm told – but even eating a few rhubarb leaves could make you feel very unwell.

Now here's the point: if you put rhubarb *leaves* in your crumble, it will taste delicious, but it will cause you harm. Gossip is just like that. Gossip tastes scrumptious, but it will harm you. Swallow enough of it and gossip can kill you – spiritually.

Proverbs 18:8 not only tells us how delicious the words of a gossip are, but it also informs us how far-reaching they are:

> The words of a gossip are like choice morsels;
>   they go down to the inmost parts.

Gossip goes down deep into us – into 'the inmost parts'.

I don't need to tell you that physiologically food goes deep down into us. After chewing our food, an involuntary muscular action called peristalsis pushes food through our digestive system. Once in our stomachs, through the digestive process, juices and enzymes break down our food, converting it into chyme which is then transferred into the small intestine, where it is turned into energy and circulated throughout our bodies.

It's a long time since I studied biology at school but I've delved into the canyons of my mind (and searched the internet!) in order to illustrate Proverbs 18:8. Just as physical food goes deep down into the inmost parts of our bodies, so gossip goes down *deep* into the inmost parts of our lives. Words of gossip go so deep into hearts and minds and souls that they infiltrate our whole lives. Gossip bores deep into church families and whole communities. Just consider how a rumour, once circulated, stays in the mind for years to come – sometimes forever. This is the poison of gossip. As we listen to gossip, it poisons our perception of people and situations and relationships.

You'll know from your own experience that, once you've heard something negative about someone (regardless of whether you know if it's true or not), it's hard to put it out of your mind. So one piece of (mis-) information can influence the way you think about a person forever. Even if gossipy words have no reliable substance, they remain in our consciousness. This is one example of James' description of the tongue as 'a restless evil, full of deadly poison' (James 3:8). The poisonous words of a gossip go down very deep to our inmost parts, just as physical food goes deep down into our physical bodies.

But one difference between food and gossip is that physiologically God has brilliantly designed the digestive system to discharge toxic waste from our bodies. By contrast, there is no natural process to eject the spiritually poisonous waste of gossip from our lives. And because there is no automatic system to get rid of the noxious effects of gossip on our hearts and minds and souls, every morsel of gossip builds up in our hearts, like toxic waste.

The poison of gossip tastes delicious, but the moment gossip leaves lips and enters ears, it's on a hazardous journey deep into hearts, souls and minds; left unchecked, it poisons us … to death.

4

GOSSIP WILL KILL YOU!

In 1971 the British government passed legislation that meant that tobacco companies had to include a government health warning on every packet of cigarettes. The warnings do not pull any punches: 'Smoking causes mouth and throat cancer.' 'Smoking causes blindness.' 'Smoking kills, quit now.' The danger of smoking is stated clearly and unequivocally. These stark warnings are deliberately designed to arrest us. Such uncompromising language might shock, but it is loving and kind to have these warnings before us. They tell us clearly the serious danger of smoking tobacco.

If gossip was sold in packs, the Bible would insist that a clear and unmissable spiritual health warning be printed in bold on the front of every packet: 'Gossip will seriously damage your spiritual health.' 'Gossip causes heart damage.' 'Gossip kills, quit now.' Gossip really is *that* dangerous. It's so dangerous that you and I need to be told, in no uncertain terms, that every time we light up a conversation with it, it poisons those who hear it.

I doubt any thoughtful Christian reading this book will want to defend or excuse the sin of gossip, but you might consider my statement that 'gossip kills' to be, well, a bit over the top. I can imagine some readers thinking, 'I know gossip is wrong, but are you really trying to tell me that it will kill me? Please don't exaggerate, Paul!'

There's much scientific and medical research to support the governments warnings about the harm tobacco does to our health. You might well wonder where's the evidence to support the deadly dangers of gossip. While you won't find a biblical proverb that states, 'Gossip kills, quit now,' let me explain how I come to such a stark conclusion.

The book of Proverbs tells us clearly that there are only two paths in life. There's the path set out by wisdom and that leads to life. The alternative path is the way of folly and it leads to death. These two ways are clearly laid out for us in the first nine chapters of Proverbs. Chapters 1–9 are the introduction to the whole book of Proverbs and the framework in which each individual proverb is to be read. From chapter 10 onwards, the book of Proverbs is full of pithy two-line sayings. These two-line gems are what generally spring to mind when we think about the book of Proverbs. But long before we get to them, the first nine chapters put each individual proverb into a very significant and important context. This context tells us that biblical proverbs are much more than just sanctified common sense. In short, each proverb gives us an opportunity to live out 'the fear of the LORD'.Chapters 1–9 are bracketed by two verses, both of which tell us the same thing:

> The fear of the LORD is the beginning of knowledge (Proverbs 1:7).

> The fear of the LORD is the beginning of wisdom (Proverbs 9:10).

The wisest thing we can do is to fear the Lord. To fear the Lord is the *beginning* of wisdom. It is not the beginning and the end of wisdom, but the starting point and foundation of all wisdom. Fear of the Lord is where all wisdom springs from.

Raymond C. Ortlund Jr writes that to fear the Lord is 'openness to him, eagerness to please him, humility to be instructed by him (Proverbs 15:33).'[1] To fear the Lord is to put Him first in our lives and above all things.[2] To fear the Lord is the wisest thing we can do, because fearing the Lord – putting Him first in our lives – is the way to have eternal life. This is life forever beyond the grave and life in all its fullness now (Proverbs 3:18 and 8:35). Fearing the Lord is the way to be saved from a life that leads to destruction.

This little book is a not a commentary on the book of Proverbs, so I can't work through the first nine chapters in great detail.[3] However, let me briefly show you how chapter 9 is a summary of the first nine chapters.

As I've already said, chapter 9 tells us that there are only two paths through life, and every human being on planet earth is on one of these. Both paths are heading somewhere. The book of Proverbs portrays us as being encouraged down those two paths by two women – with each woman trying to persuade us to walk down their particular path.

First, there's the beautiful, elegant lady 'Wisdom' (verses 1–6). Second is the seductive woman 'Folly' (verses 13–18). These two women make the same invitation: 'Let all who are simple come to my house!' (verses 4 and 16). Both women offer food to eat (verses 5 and 17). Both are calling from the highest point of the city (verses 3 and 14), suggesting that to be on their path is to reach the heights. These two women are calling us to follow them. Who we chose to follow is the most important decision we can ever make in life, because following these women leads to two very different destinations. Following the beautiful Lady Wisdom leads to life (verse 6), while following the other woman, the seductress Folly, will lead us to death (verse 18) – spiritual death.

Lady Wisdom searches for the simple (verse 4) in order to make them wise and give them life (verse 6). The woman called Folly sits and calls to those who pass by (verse 15), making fools of anyone who listens to her because her way leads to death.

Lady Wisdom offers a nutritious banquet (verse 2), but the seductress Folly offers food too (verse 17), holding out bread to us (as other Bible versions such as the ESV translate it). But as you read that, don't think of a dry, unappetising crust. Think rather of a freshly baked loaf. The bread that Folly offers is sweet and delicious (verse 17). The problem is that while her bread tastes delicious, it will kill you (verse 18). Does that ring any bells? It's what we've discovered about gossip – that it's so delicious to eat and yet so deadly to consume.

So there are two paths to follow in life – and only two. The choice is binary. Every day we make countless choices to walk down one road or the other. In our lives as a whole we have a decision to make. We can follow the beautiful Lady Wisdom and set out on her path by fearing the Lord, which is the *beginning* of wisdom (verse 10). If we chose Lady Wisdom's path, we take the road that leads to life. Alternatively, we can follow the adulterous, seductive woman Folly, by not fearing the Lord but rejecting Him. When we do that, we are on the road to hell.[4]

The opening nine chapters of the book of Proverbs set up how to read and understand the individual proverbs in the rest of the book. The first nine chapters make it blindingly obvious that the wise choice is to fear the Lord, because it leads to life – eternal life. Once I've begun the (Christian) life of wisdom – a life that begins by fearing the Lord – then the book of Proverbs encourages me to be all ears and to pay the most careful attention to live out everything Lady Wisdom tells me. Indeed, to listen to and to live by Proverbs is to demonstrate that I am an authentic follower of the Lord, on the narrow road that leads to life. Or, to use the language of Proverbs, it demonstrates that I am someone who fears the Lord. Alternatively, to put it the other way round, someone who fears the Lord will be someone who craves the words of the beautiful, elegant Lady Wisdom.

These nine chapters should also make me fearful of ignoring Proverbs because if I refuse to listen to them, then I am listening to that other woman, the scarlet woman, the seductress Folly. That is an utterly foolish way to live because following folly is to be on the road to destruction.

So listen to Lady Wisdom as she tells us:

> To fear the LORD is to hate evil;
> I hate pride and arrogance,
> evil behaviour and perverse speech.
> *(Proverbs 8:13)*

This proverb is very important for us as we consider the sin of gossip. To fear the Lord is to hate the evil that wisdom hates: 'pride and arrogance, evil behaviour and *perverse speech*' (my emphasis).

It is very striking that Lady Wisdom highlights perverse speech as something to hate. Wisdom hates the evil of speaking in a way that is unkind or unhelpful. Wisdom hates gossip – we see that here in this proverb, and we'll see it in individual proverbs in the rest of the book. To genuinely fear the Lord will result in us also hating the evil of perverse speech, like gossip. So if I don't hate perverse speech, you might quite legitimately wonder if I fear the Lord.

What's more, listen to these words from the lips of Lady Wisdom herself:

> But those who fail to find me harm themselves;
> all who hate me love death.
> *(Proverbs 8:36)*

Lady Wisdom tells me that failing to find her – and that means failing to follow her – is to love death. Failing to follow Lady Wisdom is to follow instead that other woman, Folly – and her way leads to death. So my response to the book of Proverbs is a matter of life and death.

The first nine chapters of Proverbs slap a spiritual health warning on gossip, telling me that speaking or hearing it is deadly. Gossip does me very serious spiritual harm. Consume enough of it and gossip kills. If I take this warning seriously, I'll want to cut gossip out of my life. I'll not want to gossip, and I'll not want to listen to it either.

Before wrapping up this chapter, I imagine that some people will feel very wary of what I've just written. It sounds a lot like salvation by works. It appears to jar against the gospel of grace to say, 'If you fail to live out the proverbs, you'll die spiritually.' So let me clarify.

First, the gospel of grace runs right through the Bible. We are saved by grace, through faith in Jesus Christ. We are saved through what Christ has done for us on the cross, and not through our performance or our ability to live up to a standard.

But second, throughout the Bible, a key demonstration that we are saved is the fruit we bear in our lives. As James says, 'faith without deeds is dead' (James 2:26). Looking at the way we live is an indication of whether we really have saving faith or not.

Consider this. If someone professing to be a Christian was sleeping around and deliberately ignoring the Bible command to avoid sexually immorality, I, as their pastor, would suggest to them that they were playing fast and loose with their salvation.[5] I would counsel them that to deliberately disobey God's Word in the way they conducted themselves sexually is to choose to walk away from the Lord. I would lovingly warn them that they were putting themselves in serious spiritual danger. In the language of Proverbs, I'd be concerned that they were listening to the adulterous woman Folly and on the road to destruction. Now here's the thing – what is true of deliberate and persistent sexual misconduct is also true of anyone who refuses to listen to and live out the proverbs' warnings against gossip. Jeff Robinson states this very clearly: 'Gossip can unmask the gossiper as someone who professes saving faith, but doesn't possess it.'[6]

Suddenly, putting these proverbs about gossip in their context, we see that it is critical that we perform life-saving, radical, spiritual heart surgery, and cut gossip out of our lives. It's a life-and-death issue. 'Gossip will seriously damage your spiritual health.' 'Gossip causes heart damage.' 'Gossip kills, quit now.' But just like nicotine, it's hard to quit because it's so addictive.

5

GOSSIP IS ADDICTIVE

Ricky Naputi is infamously known as 'The man who ate himself to death.'[1] He died when he was just 39 years old, weighing a whopping 900 pounds – in British 'currency', that's over 64 stone! Ricky Naputi was addicted to food and it killed him.[2] He was warned by medics that if he continued to eat the way he did, he'd die. Despite the warning, he just couldn't stop eating. Desperately, for some people, the same seems to be true when it comes to gossip. It's so addictive that they appear to be unable to stop even though it's killing them.

In the last chapter we saw that gossip seriously damages our spiritual health. If we refuse to listen to how the book of Proverbs warns us of the dangers of gossip, then we are listening to the adulterous woman Folly – and listening to her is to walk down the road to destruction. The uncomfortable truth is that failing to heed the warnings of Proverbs and refusing to deal with gossip (either individually or in a church family) suggests that we don't fear the Lord – because anyone who really has put the Lord first in their lives will want to listen to the elegant Lady Wisdom. Listening to, and then living by, the proverbs is a clear sign that we do fear the Lord.

The problem is that even if we do hear the stark warnings of the proverbs, once we've started to eat the deliciously addictive food of gossip, it is very difficult to stop. It really is *that* delicious and *that* addictive.

From chapter 13 of this book, we'll consider how to cut gossip out of our lives. But before we do that, over the next four chapters, we'll think about why we find gossip so addictive. This will help us to get to the heart issues that seems to compel us to keep gossiping. It is a critical first step so that when we begin to think about how to stop gossiping, we'll address the issue at the heart of the matter. Chapters 11 and 12 will then explore the deceitfulness of our heart but also how our heartfelt longings can be changed.

6

THE ADDICTION OF FRIENDSHIP

When we think of addiction, we usually have things like drugs, drink or gambling in mind. But we can become addicted to things that are essential for life – as was the case for Ricky Naputi with food. It's essential to eat; the problem comes when we eat too much. Now what is true of food is true of friends. It's not good to eat too many of your friends! Seriously, we can have an unhealthy need for, or reliance on, friends. Don't mishear me, though: friendship is crucial for life. We are made for relationships.

We are made in the image of the triune God, who Himself is in relationship within the Godhead. Therefore we are impoverished and less than fully human if we don't have close and meaningful friendships. Friendship is a great gift from God. More than that, friendship is essential if we're to flourish in life. But when friendship becomes *too* important to us, we can get ourselves into all sorts of problems. When friendship becomes more than it should, we can be tempted to do *anything* to gain friends – and that 'anything' includes gossip. It's this desperate desire for friendship that makes gossip such an attractive and addictive option for some – because they think gossip will win them friends, and having friends is more important to them than obeying God. Such people are addicted to friendship.

But gossip, rather than gaining us good friends, ruins friendships. And even when gossip succeeds in attracting people to hang around us, it doesn't help us form friendships with the right kind of people.

Next time you're out with a group of people and there's a lull in the conversation, try this test. Lean forward, lower your voice and say, 'Can I tell you a secret?' I can almost guarantee you that you'll instantly have everyone's attention. Your mates will be on the edge of their seats – metaphorically and quite possibly literally – as they lean in to listen to what you have to tell them.

If you're out with just one other person, glance over your shoulder (as if checking that no-one else is in earshot), look very earnest and then say to your friend, 'I have something to tell you, but let's keep this just between you and me…' If I were a betting man, I'd put big money on your companion being all ears.

Being in possession of a piece of information that mustn't go any further is remarkably magnetic. We all love to be in the loop and so we love to hear the latest intel. People love to hear the latest tittle-tattle. Since gossip tastes so good, like choice morsels, dishing out gossip is like handing out sweets in a school playground – it makes you very popular.

So one reason some people are tempted to gossip is because they think it will make them popular and get them friends. If they keep dishing out delicious morsels, others will want to hang out with them, won't they? Gossip appears to gain us friends.

At the beginning of this book I told you how, in 30 years of pastoral ministry, no-one has ever confessed to me the sin of gossip. However, there was one man – let's call him Gary[1] – who did admit to me that he was a gossip. That wasn't news to me – I knew he was a gossiper, as did others who knew him well. What was novel was to hear him acknowledge and admit to being one. But here's the strange thing: when Gary admitted to being a gossip, he wasn't confessing his sin to me but justifying it! Sometime later, when I heard Gary say that he idolised friendship, his compulsive, excessive and destructive gossiping begun to make sense to me. His desperate need for everyone to be his friend was like a drug to him. He felt that having all the latest gossip was a means to making, and then keeping, the friends he so desperately craved. But the wisdom of Proverbs tells us something very revealing.

While we think that gossip will make us friends, Proverbs tell us that gossip breaks friendships:

> A perverse person stirs up conflict,
> and a gossip separates close friends.
> *(Proverbs 16:28)*

There are a number of things to learn from this proverb.

First, note that the Bible's assessment of gossip is that it is perverse. The second line of a proverb often helps us to understand the first. So the second line of this proverb tells us that the gossiper it describes is the perverse person in the first line. Second, note that gossip is never an incidental thing – it stirs up conflict. A gossiper is someone who causes problems.

Third, see that gossip separates close friendship. At one level, it's obvious how that happens. If a close friend gossips about you, it will put distance between you. Therefore Gary, who gossiped out of a desire to attract friends, was losing the friendship of every person he gossiped about. But I wonder too if it ever crossed Gary's mind that his gossiping was actually losing him the *close* friendships he *really needed* – namely the friendship of *wise* friends.

That is because every time we gossip to wise people, they'll want to avoid us. That's also the wisdom of Proverbs:

> A gossip betrays a confidence;
> so avoid anyone who talks too much.
> *(Proverbs 20:19)*

I find that very striking. When you're tempted to buddy up with a gossiper by listening to their tittle-tattle, you are putting yourself in a relationship with someone who is likely to betray your confidence.

A few months back, I was planning an initiative that needed to remain confidential at the time. Another person in church leadership had generously pledged to financially support this venture. However, I felt unable to share some developments with our benefactor because, in the past, he had often tried to share things with me about others that he really shouldn't have divulged. As a result, I didn't feel sure that he would be able to keep this information to himself! I kept information from him and kept him at arm's length. I did that because Proverbs tells us that it's wise to distance ourselves from people who have a gossip problem.

Lady Wisdom advises me:

> A gossip betrays a confidence,
> but a trustworthy person keeps a secret.
> *(Proverbs 11:13)*

> Walk with the wise and become wise,
> for a companion of fools suffers harm.
> *(Proverbs 13:20)*

As Lady Wisdom says, avoid a gossiper. When someone tries to share the latest gossip with me, I'd be wise not only to stop them – because it will poison me – but to *avoid* them too. I would certainly be wise not to have them as a close friend.

Now do you see how gossiping Gary was shooting himself in the foot? He gossiped in order to gain friends, but his gossiping lost him *wise* friends. The 'friends' he did attract to him through his gossiping were not the kind of wise friends Gary needed to help him walk faithfully with the Lord. Gary needed people around him to tell him to stop gossiping, not those who wanted to listen to his tittle-tattle.

In his excellent little book *True Friendship* Vaughan Roberts writes, 'Wisdom may ... require not just the making of friends but, in some cases, the breaking of them – or at least the loosening of ties.' He adds, 'our closest friends should be those who share our highest goals and help us live up to them.'[2]

Those who gossip in order to get friends lose the very friends they need. They need wise friends who will help them to stop gossiping, but wise people avoid them. I'm sure the irony is not lost on you. The gossiper who longs to gain friends through their gossiping does precisely the opposite. Even if their gossiping surrounds them with people, they won't have the wise close friends they need who are prepared to help them live and grow in their fear of the Lord.

7

THE ADDICTION OF POWER AND CONTROL

People can get their pets to do the most amazing tricks. In 2012 Ashleigh Butler won *Britain's Got Talent* with her dog, Pudsey – a Border Collie, Brichon Frise and Chinese Crested powderpuff cross (that's quite a mouthful!).

Training a dog takes hours and hours of patient endurance ... and an endless supply of delicious treats. My simple (and arguably too simplistic) understanding is that the incentive for pets to obey commands is a tasty morsel. Dogs will do what you want them to if you reward them with a scrummy snack.

Gossips operate with a not dissimilar strategy. They think they can control people by dishing out choice morsels. As we've already seen, sadly their strategy can work because gossip tastes so good. So gossipers endlessly sniff out the latest info in order to acquire the titbits they need to gain control over others. Control-hungry gossips are desperate to be the first to know about an engagement or a pregnancy or a marriage break-up. They want to be the first to spread news. They also love to be in possession of confidential information or an announcement that has been embargoed. Having that information gives them a feeling of power and a sense that they have everything they need to control others.[1] That feeling is heightened when they contact a friend and whisper the most enticing beginning to any sentence: 'You must not tell anyone but…' Such a delicious start to a conversation gives the gossiper a very real feeling of being in control of those around them. And it works (or at least it gives the gossiper a sense of control) as many people, like performing dogs, keep coming back for another tasty morsel.

To return to the book of Proverbs, the opening sentence tells us that the author (of a large portion of the book) is King Solomon:

> The proverbs of Solomon son of David, king of Israel (Proverbs 1:1).

As we read on, we discover that King Solomon was writing the book of Proverbs for his son(s), who he instructs again and again:

> Listen, my son, to your father's instruction
> (Proverbs 1:8).[2]

So here is a king – the anointed King of Israel – addressing his sons. The King of Israel, like any king of the day, was hugely powerful and had control over many. But with that kind of power comes a real danger. As that well-known saying goes – a saying that is most often attributed to Lord Acton – 'Power tends to corrupt, and absolute power corrupts absolutely.' The King of Israel and his sons, who of course were princes – one of whom would be the next King of Israel, could very easily be corrupted by the power of their exalted position. Therefore Proverbs is written by King Solomon to urge his sons to live in a way that does not abuse their power. They were to fear the Lord and live in a way that reflected this. They were to acknowledge that the Lord is in control; that the Lord has all ultimate power and authority in the world. In the introduction to the book of Proverbs, Lady Wisdom says of herself:

> By me kings reign
>   and rulers issue decrees that are just;
> by me princes govern,
>   and nobles – all who rule on earth.
> *(Proverbs 8:15–16)*

In other words, Solomon, who was considered to be one of the wisest men on the planet,[3] instructs his sons that they were to rule by wisdom. Wisdom is at the heart of godly ruling and reigning. Kings are to reign *by wisdom* in making just laws. The words 'By me' at the start of this extract are clearly Lady Wisdom speaking because of how she begins this particular speech in the preceding verses:

> I, wisdom, dwell together with prudence;
> I possess knowledge and discretion.
> To fear the LORD is to hate evil;
> I hate pride and arrogance,
> evil behaviour and perverse speech.
> Counsel and sound judgment are mine;
> I have insight, I have power.
> *(Proverbs 8:12–14)*

Solomon urges his sons to have wisdom at the heart of their ruling and governance, and here he says that wisdom is about prudence, knowledge and discretion (verse 12), and about the fear of the Lord (verse 13). And fearing the Lord (the beginning of wisdom) means hating – yes, it's that strong – evil, pride, arrogance, evil behaviour and perverse speech (verse 13). Each of these qualities deserves unhurried, thoughtful reflection, but for our purposes in this book we will focus on how the last in the list – perverse speech – is to be hated by those who fear the Lord.

Wisdom tells the sons of Solomon, the future leaders of Israel, not to try to control people through perverse speech – and that includes gossip. It is perverse to attempt to control others through gossip. Gossip is a gross misuse of power and an abuse of others. It's an evil we should hate. So why do we gossip? It is because power and control are very addictive.

In the 1944 Memorial Lecture at King's College, London, C. S. Lewis, the Oxford don and author of *The Chronicles of Narnia*, warned his audience of the danger of what he called 'the inner ring'. The inner ring is any influential group of people of which we really want to be a part. Being in the inner ring makes us feel included and helps us feel empowered – especially when that inner ring is a group of movers and shakers in an organisation (like a church). Being in the inner ring makes us feel accepted and important and powerful. And longing for power and position and a place at the table will strongly motivate us to gossip.

Here's how C. S. Lewis put it in his lecture:

> I believe that in all men's lives at certain periods, and in many men's lives at all periods between infancy and extreme old age, one of the most dominant elements is the desire to be inside the local Ring and the terror of being left outside.

We are desperate to be included. At one level this is entirely understandable. We are made in the image of the trinitarian God who, at His heart, is in loving relationship. We need to be in relationship. We were made to be in relationship. But being fallen creatures, we want more than inclusion in community – we desperately want to be at the centre of the community, even controlling the community. That longing to control others comes from a desire to be in God's place – and that is a very ugly and destructive desire indeed.

So the motivation to gossip comes from a desire to be at the centre of everything and to feel as if we're controlling things – or at least to have some measure of influence over others. Some believe that gossip will give them a pass into the *inner* ring, or even better, enable them to create an inner ring. Then, once they're part of this inner ring, gossip appears to be their trump card to gaining the centre ground in that exclusive and powerful group of people. Such people gossip out of the belief that it is the vehicle to get them places.

It's widely thought that those who strive for power are trying to overcome feelings of powerlessness. Control is their way of compensating for feelings of insecurity. The desire for power and control is essentially a defence against feelings of inadequacy, weakness, fear and worthlessness. Feelings of power and control mask those crushing feelings of inadequacy and worthlessness.

Many church leaders will have experienced people like this. Imagine Gabrielle – or Gabby for short. She seems to know everybody's business. Meet her and she'll ask you lots of questions. She appears to be genuinely interested in you and your well-being, but as time goes on, you begin to realise she's actually trying to get information out of you. Gabby especially loves to tell her friends what church leaders have told her. All this is because she needs to be in possession of, and then dish out, information in order to feel as if she is Someone. Her need to control springs from a deep insecurity.

If any of this is connecting with you, please see the danger of needing to be in control. A desperation for power and control destroys. J. R. R. Tolkien demonstrated it brilliantly in his fantasy trilogy *Lord of the Rings*. The desire for power transformed Sméagol, a joyful hobbit, into Gollum, a monster with a twisted body and mind.

So gossip can be a form of control. If I have information, I feel empowered. That's why some people like to discover information and dish it out, and why others love to hear it.

Gossip is also a way of controlling people by putting them in their place. Spreading information that should be kept confidential, or spreading misinformation or harmful information about someone, lowers the status of our rival and gives us a feeling of control over them.

But Proverbs helps us think quite differently when it comes to power and control:

> In their hearts humans plans their course,
> but the LORD establishes their steps.
> (Proverbs 16:9)

We may feel as if we're in control. We make our plans. But no matter how much we plot and plan, the Lord is in control of our ways – and the ways of everyone else on the planet. So while in our sinful, scheming hearts we plot and plan, trying to engineer any number of outcomes, that is such a foolish way to live. The Lord establishes all steps – both our steps and the steps of anyone we choose to gossip about. Don't be fooled into thinking that you are powerful enough, or in control enough, to be able to impact the outcome of someone else's life. That is certainly something we need to grasp when we think about the next addiction.

8

THE ADDICTION OF REVENGE

Gavin wanted to get even. As an onlooker, it seemed to me that he hadn't actually been badly treated, but he felt that he had. He had worked for the same organisation for years, but a change of management resulted in him becoming increasingly frustrated. He didn't like the direction the organisation was moving in and he didn't feel that he fitted in any more. However, he didn't want to just walk away and get another job. He'd given so much of his life to this establishment and he felt like he belonged there. So he stuck with it until he could stand it no longer, and then he handed in his notice. He said he felt pushed out, although, as he told me his story, I don't think anyone actually pushed him anywhere.

During his three-month notice period he told as many people as possible why he was leaving. His narrative included derogatory stories about the management. He spoke of his line manager and the head of department as harsh people who had made his life a misery. In truth they were fair – they just ran things differently to how it used to be done, and how Gavin felt it should be done.

The problem was that as Gavin gossiped his narrative, it caused havoc. Many people listened to him because he'd been part of the organisation for such a long time. Before Gavin started his vengeful gossiping, the organisation had been a happy place to work. Now, a number of people sided with him and some jumped on the gossiping bandwagon too. By the time Gavin left, there were all manner of rumours flying around the organisation.

Gavin didn't consider his rumour mongering inappropriate. Indeed, when he was challenged about it by a Christian friend, he justified his gossip. 'It was important to expose the management,' he said. In truth, he was seeking revenge.

George handled things quite differently. He'd been badly treated. His reputation was trashed and his life turned upside down. George was a humble guy who took criticism seriously. Anyone who knew George realised that the things said about him were unfair and blown out of all proportion. George admitted that he hadn't got everything right (who does?). The low-key HR investigation into what he'd allegedly done agreed that there were things he could have done differently, but concluded that he was free to continue in his role. But the whole episode left George with a significant loss of confidence. Also, because his adversary had freely gossiped about him, he didn't know who knew what or who believed what about him, and so he felt he had to leave his job.

As the months went by, George tried to 'move on', but he found his mind racing and often plotting an ugly course of revenge. But unlike Gavin, George was honest with himself. He admitted the vengeful feelings for what they were and asked Christian friends to help him fight the temptation to get even.

George told me, 'At times, getting even was all I could think about. Every day, day after day, and many times throughout the day – every day for months – I turned over what had been said about me. I felt I'd been robbed of my career. Even though I was cleared of any serious wrong doing, I felt my reputation was in tatters. I was hurting and so was my family. So every day I found myself plotting how I could pay back those who had done this to me. I knew I should forgive. I knew it would be better for me to just let it go. I knew I should leave retribution to God. I knew that justice would be done one day. But "one day" seemed a long time to wait. I wanted those who had caused me such pain to pay for it now. I wanted them to get a taste of their own medicine.'

So although George had been badly treated, he held his tongue and fought the powerful urge to tell his side of the story. He bit his tongue even though, as he said,

'At times it seemed to take all the energy I could muster to say nothing.'

The desire to exact revenge is extremely strong. If someone has hurt you, you want to pay them back. Maybe a work colleague steals your idea and then undermines you in front of your boss. Perhaps someone spreads a rumour about you that's just not true. Or possibly a friend spills the beans and tells others something that you had told them in confidence.

The American singer-songwriter Taylor Swift knows all about the power of desiring to get even. In her song 'Look what you made me do' she writes that although the world is quick to move on to the next gossip, she can only think about karma.[1] Her powerful lyrics express a powerful emotion. When I feel wronged and hurt, I can't move on. Revenge is all I think about. I'm gonna get you back. You've got it coming to you. You've done me wrong and I'm gonna make sure that retribution comes your way.

This desire to get even may dissipate over time, but unchecked it can fester like an open wound until the need for revenge becomes a toxic obsession. If we're not careful, it can consume us and infect us so seriously that it destroys us inside. Or, to change the metaphor, we can feel the need for revenge like an addict needs a fix. When it takes root, it's all we can think about.

Of course, there are any number of ways we can try to get even, but most of us (Christian or not) won't engage in the type of vengeful retaliation that grabs headlines or warrants prison time. However, we *can* plot the downfall of our 'enemies' through spreading malicious gossip designed to exact revenge. And gossip, especially when it's on social media, is like throwing a rock into a still lake – the ripples spread far and wide. Gossip is a very effective way to get even.Revenge is about making my enemy feel pain. I want them to feel something of the pain they have inflicted on me. Revenge feels like justice. They hurt me; I have the right to hurt them – an eye for an eye, a tooth for a tooth. But it's not that simple. As we've seen already, when you gossip in order to hurt someone else, you are killing yourself.

Of course, 'getting even' is off limits for the Christian for so many reasons:

> Do not say, 'I'll pay you back for this wrong!'
> Wait for the Lord, and he will avenge you.
> *(Proverbs 20:22)*

The Lord says, 'It is mine to avenge' (Deuteronomy 32:35; Romans 12:19). One of the wonderful things about the gospel is that we know that God *will* put right all wrongs, one day. We *can* leave God to bring about justice. Jesus is our great example in this, on the cross:

> When they hurled their insults at him, he did not retaliate; when he suffered, he made no threats. Instead, he entrusted himself to him who judges justly (1 Peter 2:23).

Jesus didn't fight back – not even with words. As we look at Jesus' example, let's be clear that saying nothing when we are badly misrepresented takes incredible strength and self-control. Jesus of course was both strong and self-controlled, and what enabled Him to live this way was the knowledge that He could trust His Heavenly Father to deal justly with all wrongs. But when we're hurting, it's hard to wait until that future judgement day, and so it's incredibly hard to say nothing.

That is why Proverbs urges:

> Do not say, I'll do to them as they have done to me;
> I'll pay them back for what they did.
> *(Proverbs 24:29)*

One of the things I love about the Bible is how God's Word knows me inside out. This proverb precisely describes my heart response when I've been badly treated. My guess is that if you've been hurt, or if you feel you've been mistreated, you have plotted your revenge too. If that's true of you, then reread Proverbs 24:29 and remember that as you plot your revenge, the adulterous woman Folly is luring you down a path of death. Rather than listen to that foolish temptress, listen instead to the beautiful Lady Wisdom, who wants to lead you in the path of life. She says, 'Do not say … "I'll pay them back."' Yes, spreading incriminating information against enemies will taste delicious and will feel incredibly satisfying at the time, but it will poison you. Rather than bringing things to a good and fair conclusion, it's likely to result in them escalating:

> Hatred stirs up conflict (Proverbs 10:12).

We can think that getting revenge will stop someone from hurting us again. We may think that if we pay people back, it will send a strong signal that we're not someone to be messed with. We might think that getting even will bring things to a conclusion – a conclusion that will be good for me. However, the hatred of revenge doesn't bring things to an end, but rather stirs up conflict – quite possibly inciting our enemy to retaliate. Then, rather than bringing things to a conclusion, the hatred behind revenge escalates the conflict – provoking people to throw more mud back in our direction.

So don't retaliate. Don't retaliate in any way. This includes not retaliating with gossip, because:

> Without wood a fire goes out;
> without a gossip a quarrel dies down.
> *(Proverbs 26:20)*

Gossiping is like pouring paraffin on a fire. Gossip as a means to revenge will stoke the fire – it will turn the heat up. So instead of retaliating with gossip, respond with loving words and kind actions:

Hatred stirs up conflict,
but love covers over all wrongs.
(Proverbs 10:12)

Now we're talking. This is radical Christian discipleship. This is following in the footsteps of Jesus. Rather than responding in revenge, we're to love.

To his credit, George tried to live that way. It wasn't easy. As George said to me, 'So often I wanted to tell the world my side of the story and how badly I'd been treated.' It was incredibly tough for George to refuse to take revenge. But by not retaliating, the painful situation he'd endured didn't escalate further. If only Gavin had learnt that lesson.

9

THE ADDICTION OF JEALOUSY

Jealousy is a very powerful emotion; left unchecked, it drives people to extremes. Studies have shown that jealousy is a huge motive for homicides – particularly in domestic violence cases.[1] Some jealous husbands will stop at nothing to avenge their wives' infidelity.

The book of Proverbs warns us of the power of jealousy:

> Anger is cruel and fury overwhelming,
> but who can stand before jealousy?
> *(Proverbs 27:4)*

The first line of this proverb observes how people can do all sorts of terrible things when they're in a fit of rage. When the red mist descends, all good judgement goes out of the window. But then the second line of the proverb tells us that while anger and rage are overwhelming, jealousy takes things to another level altogether. Jealousy can be more overwhelming than a person who's been overcome by anger.

Of course, most people don't allow jealousy to drive them to physically kill someone else, just as most people don't allow their anger to lead them to murder, but jealousy can very quickly lead to character assassination. It is sometimes jealousy that gives people the overwhelming desire to hurt someone with gossip. It might be that jealousy is behind the desire for revenge that we considered in the last chapter.

Gore Vidal, the American writer and intellectual, is widely thought to have been the first to say, 'Every time a friend succeeds, I die a little.' Do you know that feeling of being jealous of a friend's success? It's horrible, but that's what jealousy does – it corrodes you at your core.

Listen again to Lady Wisdom:

> A heart at peace gives life to the body,
> but envy rots the bones.
> *(Proverbs 14:30)*

If envy is not dealt with it, it rots us like an old wooden bench that's left out in all weathers. Envy and jealousy makes us rotten right down to the bones – our bones being the structure that keeps us standing. Let jealousy get a hold and it will ruin life – your life will crumble because jealousy will eat away at the very foundation of who you are. It will motivate you to ruin the life of others too.

The rot of jealousy eats away at us. So we'd do well to spot its first signs. When you find yourself irritated because someone else is celebrated or applauded, jealousy is taking root. When you fantasise about the failure of a successful colleague, jealousy has begun to rot your soul. When you're smugly delighted to hear of a hardship or difficulty coming upon another who has been successful, it's a sign that you're jealous of them. Beware when these signs of jealousy appear in the heart because, unless you're a quite extraordinary human being, it's only a short step to plotting your adversaries' downfall – and your plot might well involve trashing their reputation through gossip.

Raymond Ortlund asks:

> Who can stand against jealousy? It will keep coming after you relentlessly, until you come down to its level. If you refuse to knuckle under, it will punish you – and blame you for it all.[2]

Ortlund understands what Lady Wisdom has been telling us – that if we follow the adulterous woman Folly, she will ruin us. Make no mistake: in the process of trying to assassinate the character of another, we kill ourselves.

Gossip is a way of leaving an adversary in a very bad light. Even in this age of fake news, many don't feel the need to fact-check whether the information received is completely true or not. Malicious gossip doesn't need to tell the whole story – just a half-truth will do. Even when we tell the truth, just putting forward one side of the story (our side) can be very persuasive – after all, no-one can deny how I 'feel'. Let's be clear that when we tell our side of the story, we are only telling *one* side – and often one side of the story is only half the truth, not the whole truth. As Jim Packer brilliantly cautions us,

> 'A half-truth treated as the whole truth becomes a complete untruth.'[3]

When telling our side of the story presents a half-truth, we are lying. I imagine we all know that when we retell a story, we cast ourselves as the hero – or at least portray ourselves in the best possible light. As we tell our side of the story, we're often convinced it's the full picture because our inner lawyer[4] is absolutely brilliant at arguing our case and persuading us that we're innocent – or at least not guilty. We additionally have an inner publicist who writes the best review on our performance, so that we convince ourselves that the world could barely exist without us. So, every time we tell our story, it is invariably highly biased in our favour.

Let's be careful here of the consequences. Telling our story can be very dangerous because it's so powerful. Nor in our current culture does it seem that anyone is permitted to challenge how we feel, especially if we cast ourselves in the role of victim.

In short, we need to face up to the fact that giving 'one side of the story' is rarely (if ever) the whole truth and can be extremely incriminating. If I gossip my side of the story, in no time at all a character is assassinated – condemned by people who love to be judge and jury, without ever hearing all the evidence.

When I was discussing this book with a publisher, he insightfully pointed out how quickly we draw conclusions even when we don't have all the information. Once we come to our conclusion, we start talking about what we've heard as if we've weighed all the information (even though we're not even in possession of all the facts). Then we speak authoritatively as if our conclusion and judgements are right, final and just.

Once again we'd do well to turn to Lady Wisdom as she highlights the danger of coming to conclusions based on the first thing we hear:

> The first to plead his case seems right,
> Until another comes and examines him.
>
> *(Proverbs 18:17, NASB)*

We should be slow to rush to conclusions. We are not God and rarely (if ever) have access to all the facts. We should look carefully at our hearts and our motives before swallowing whole what we're told. And we should certainly be extremely cautious of passing on information we've heard from another.

In summary, beware of the destructive power of jealousy or you'll find yourself saying all manner of devastating things in order to hurt others, whether it's true or not.

10

PAUSE FOR THOUGHT

In the last four chapters we've been considering why we gossip. In the chapters that follow we'll move towards getting rid of gossip from our lives and fellowships. But it's crucial we stop and consider the issues in these last chapters before we jump to trying to stop our gossiping. We need to come to an understanding of why we personally gossip. We need to understand the motives of our hearts. That said, understanding our hearts is a really difficult thing because, as we've already noted, Jeremiah tells us:

> The heart is deceitful above all things and desperately wicked: who can know it? (Jeremiah 17:9, KJV).

Our hearts will deceive us. Our inner lawyer always comes to our defence and justifies our actions – even when our actions have been very ugly. Our inner publicist is brilliant at convincing us to believe our own publicity. So please reflect honestly on these last chapters as we've considered the addictions of a damaged heart that so powerfully urges us to gossip.

We must start with this kind of honest self-examination and heart diagnostic otherwise we'll find ourselves unable to stop gossiping – because of the strong addictive heart problems of jealousy, revenge, control or an unhealthy need of friendship. So before you read on, let me ask you to be as honest with yourself as you can. Are you like Gary who's desperate for friends? Or perhaps you identify with Gabby who wants to be in control. Maybe Gavin's or George's stories of wanting revenge connected with you. Is it possible that you can see that you're being eaten up with jealousy? It might be that there's another reason for your gossiping – something I've not addressed. For example, your inappropriate speech might be the result of a lack of self-control, which means that you thoughtlessly talk too much.[1]

Please take some time to examine your heart. Pray that the Lord would help you to put your finger on why you gossip. Then be determined to think through how the gospel deals with your heart issue. You may need to sit down with a wise Christian to help you with this. Be sure to pray that the Holy Spirit would give you the desire to change, and as you do, know that the Holy Spirit will empower you to change.[2]

Personal reflection

11

THE WAY OF WISDOM

By this point in this book, I hope you're itching to rid your life of gossip. I hope you're convinced that gossip is a serious problem that really does need to be weeded out of our lives and frowned upon in our churches. If so, you might now be wanting me to spell out for you an ABC of eradicating gossip. Of course it's not that simple. Even if it were, we're not quite ready for that yet. We will consider steps to stop gossiping in chapter 13, but before that we need to understand more the complexity and deceitfulness of our heart.

So far we've seen how gossip tastes so irresistibly delicious – despite its destructive, poisonous, lethal consequences. In chapters 5–9 we explored addictions that compel us to gossip. Now, in this chapter and the next, we'll look further at the heart. In this chapter we'll consider that our fallen state causes us to have a highly distorted view of how wise we are. Our twisted understanding even convinces us that we know better than God! So even though God tells us not to gossip, we actually believe, in our flawed wisdom, that gossip will be good for us and help us prosper.

Ever since the first human, Adam, was placed in the Garden of Eden, we have wanted to decide what is right and wrong. Simply trusting God's Word is not enough for us. In Genesis 2, the Lord God said to Adam, 'you must not eat from the tree of the knowledge of good and evil for when you eat from it you will certainly die' (Genesis 2:17). But Adam didn't trust God. Adam thought he knew best. Adam swallowed the snake's lie that God was robbing him of the opportunity to be wise: 'God knows that when you eat from it [the tree of the knowledge of good and evil] your eyes will be opened, and you will be like God, knowing good and evil' (Genesis 3:5).

The snake convinced Eve and Adam that eating the forbidden fruit would not result in death (Genesis 3:4), even though God clearly stated that it would (Genesis 2:17). When Eve looked at the forbidden tree, she concluded that it was 'desirable for gaining wisdom' (Genesis 3:6), and so she ate the fruit of the tree in order to become wise. But one of the most devastating moments in the Fall narrative is that Genesis 3:6 also tells us that while Eve was being tempted by the snake, Adam was standing alongside her the entire time: 'She also gave some to her husband, *who was with her*, and he ate it' (emphasis mine).

The first humans believed that doing things their way would enhance their lives. They thought they knew best – and better than God. Adam and Eve were wise in their own eyes. When we put it that starkly, we can see what utter fools Adam and Eve were. But let me caution you before you write them off as the biggest plonkers who ever walked planet earth. The bare, and rather uncomfortable, truth is that we too think we know best. And very often we believe that even when God says differently. Throughout our lifetime, every one of us makes a gazillion decisions to follow a course of action that we think is wise, even when it's not in line with God's Word.

The lives of Adam and Eve are a paradigm of ours, and their disobedience in the Garden of Eden is the biblical backdrop to wisdom in the Bible. We ignore God's Word because we think we can figure out what will happen if we take this, that or another course of action. This is pompous pride. What on earth makes us think that we can know how things will work out? Just reflect on that for a moment. How many times have you made a decision and things have *not* happened the way you expected?

To illustrate what nonsense and utter foolishness it is to think this way, let me transport you back to the end of 2019. As you were making your plans for the year ahead, did you for one minute think the world would be in the grip of a global pandemic in 2020? If I'd known that Covid-19 would grip the world as it did, I'd have bought shares in Zoom and quadrupled my investment in just 10 months! We don't know how things are going to turn out.

Putting aside big issues like global pandemics, we don't know what's round the corner even in our own lives. How many times have you said, or heard others say, 'If only I'd known what would happen, I'd have never…' But God does. God knows everything – and *only* God knows everything. Only God is in possession of all the facts – past, present and future. Only He can see how things will pan out if we take a particular course of action.

In short, God is all-knowing and wise, and we are not. And it's precisely because of our lack of wisdom that the book of Proverbs says:

> Trust in the LORD with all your heart
> and lean not on your own understanding;
> in all your ways submit to him,
> and he will make your paths straight.Do not be wise
> in your own eyes;
> fear the LORD and shun evil.
> *(Proverbs 3:5–7)*

'Trust in the LORD with all your heart.' With every ounce of trust you can muster up in your heart, trust what the Lord says. Trust what He says throughout the Bible. Not least of all, trust what He says in the book of Proverbs. Don't lean 'on your own understanding'. You may think a course of action or a decision will be good for you, but if God's Word says differently – if a biblical proverb says otherwise – don't 'be wise in your own eyes'. Consider yourself a simpleton – that's the counsel of

Lady Wisdom (Proverbs 9:4). Consider yourself someone who knows next to nothing. Rather than having a high view of yourself, 'fear the LORD and shun evil' – including the evil of gossip. Proverbs tells us to give up all claims to being wise. Indeed, a great mark of wisdom is realising how much we don't know!

Until we really believe we're not that wise, we will persuade ourselves that sometimes gossip is good for us. We may think that spreading gossip will buy us friends and make us popular and so make us happy. We might reason that spreading a piece of misinformation or half-truth will be good for us in one way or another. By putting someone else down, perhaps that will result in us being elevated – maybe we'll been seen in a better light; it might even give us power, a foot in the door or a promotion. We imagine that getting revenge through gossiping will show our adversary that we're not to be trifled with and give us control. But the Lord is clear that it's never good to gossip or hang out with a gossiper:

> Whoever .... spreads slander is a fool (Proverbs 10:18).

We have to trust the Lord's wisdom because sometimes (dare I say, often?) we think His commands don't appear to be the smart move.

As we plot and plan, we reason that gossiping will make things better for us. But, as we've already seen, God's Word says that if you shun evil, including gossip, 'he will make your paths straight' (Proverbs 3:6). This is not a promise that everything in our lives will be trouble-free, but a promise that we'll be on the straight and narrow path that leads to life (Matthew 7:13–14). As we've also seen, if we ignore the call of Lady Wisdom, we will be walking down the crooked path to destruction. So trust the Lord and His Word because that's the only way to avoid walking down the path of the seductive woman Folly – a path that always leads to death. In short, your own understanding will kill you, just as it killed Adam and every human who came after him.

It's as if the Lord says, 'Every time you think that gossip is going to make things better for you, trust me. Don't listen to the snake, or his sidekick – that seductress woman, Folly. And don't think that you're smart enough to work out how things are going to pan out if you follow your way.'

Only when we believe that God is wise and we're *not* wise will we be ready and willing to listen to the proverbs.

12

THE HEART OF THE MATTER

Telling a gossip to stop gossiping is a bit like telling an alcoholic to stop drinking. Gossip is so delicious and so addictive that just being told to 'stop it' won't bring long and lasting change. Likewise, even if you're longing to cut gossip out of your life, simply telling yourself to 'try harder', or to 'bite your tongue', or to 'count to ten before you speak' – or any other piece of self-help advice – won't be enough to change the habit of a lifetime. What we need is heart change. We need transformation at the deepest and most profound level. We need a work of the Holy Spirit to bring about in us a deep longing *not* to be a gossip, or associate with gossips, or ever listen to gossip. In this chapter we'll see that deep heartfelt longing to change comes through a fear of the Lord.

> …through the fear of the Lord evil is avoided (Proverbs 16:6).

I love this proverb. In chapter 4 of this book we considered how the fear of the Lord is the big point of Proverbs, the foundation of all wisdom and the context for all the proverbs. The proverb above states clearly that we will have a fighting chance of living out the individual proverbs through having a fear of the Lord.

Let me take you back to those key verses in proverbs:

> The fear of the Lord is the beginning of knowledge (Proverbs 1:7).

> The fear of the Lord is the beginning of wisdom (Proverbs 9:10).

Now look closely at the next line of Proverbs 1:7:

> …but fools despise wisdom and instruction.

I have mentioned before that the second line of a proverb often sheds light on the first. Here we see that the antithesis of fearing the Lord is to despise wisdom – to have contempt for or to be aloof to wisdom. It is to consider ourselves too clever to listen to wisdom. To think we know best, as we were considering in the last chapter.

Sadly, despite all we've seen about the dangers of gossip, some people reading this will *still* be thinking it's not that bad, or it can't do that much harm, or it might even be the smart thing to do. If that's you, then I can't help you. And if that is you, don't kid yourself that you can keep your gossip under control. It will destroy other people, and you too.

But for those who have been challenged to change and eradicate gossip from your lives, you need both a hatred of the sin of gossip and to love God more than you love sin. Proverbs 16:6 describes this great love of God as a fear of the Lord. When we fear the Lord, we'll be eager to please Him. We'll love Him more than the delicious taste of gossip. As another proverb teaches us:

> The fear of the LORD is a fountain of life,
> turning a person from the snares of death.
> *(Proverbs 14:27)*

As we increasingly fear the Lord, we will want to listen to and live out what Proverbs teach us. Michael Reeves explains, 'The fear of the Lord consumes sinful desires and fuels holy ones.'[1]

Fearing the Lord changes my heart, and it is heart change that leads to changed lives.

Some years back, a student asked me to keep him accountable in his relationship with his girlfriend. As we chatted about sexual boundaries, he said to me, 'My dad told me that the only way I'll remain sexually pure is if I love God more than I love sex.' What a wise dad. Having boundaries and rules and asking other Christians to keep us accountable can be extremely helpful, but at the end of the day, there's one wonderfully powerful motivation to live as we should – a love of God. Or, as Proverbs would put it, a 'fear of the Lord'.

If we just give ourselves a list of dos and don'ts, that won't be enough when the delicious temptation to gossip comes (especially when we're tired, or scared, or think we're being wise). We won't have the resolve to keep our rules and will slip back into those old habits of gossiping, or listening to gossip. Fear of the Lord, on the other hand, gives us a longing to please Him. And with the help of the Holy Spirit, we have a fighting chance of not just avoiding gossip, but actually hating gossip:

> To fear the LORD is to hate evil;
> I hate pride and arrogance,
> evil behaviour and perverse speech.
> *(Proverbs 8:13)*

Listen again to Michael Reeves, who so clearly understands the transforming power of the fear of the Lord:

> [The fear of the Lord] consumes sinful desires and fuels holy ones. And the word 'desires' there is key, for … the fear of the Lord does not keep believers from sin in the sense that it makes us merely alter our behaviour for fear of punishment. Rather, it brings us to *adore* God and so loathe sin and long to be truly and thoroughly like him.[2]

This is what makes real Christian faith so different from religion. Religion gives us rules to live by, but rules are powerless to change us deep down. The fear of the Lord, on the other hand, gives us a deep-down heart desire to stop gossiping.

May I suggest that as you consider putting things in place to stop gossiping, you write at the top of your prayer list: 'Desire to fear the Lord.' Make it a daily prayer for the Lord to give you a heart that loves Him more than anything else. Ask Him to bring you to a place where He rules your heart. Beg Him to make your greatest fear that of hurting Him, disappointing Him or denying Him – not because your salvation depends on you living up to a certain standard, but as a response to His grace. Ask Him to make you so thrilled to have been saved by Jesus that you want to love Him with all your heart, all your soul, all your mind and all your strength.

As the Lord answers that prayer, and the desires of our heart change, we'll be better equipped to put out the fire of gossip in our lives.

13

PUTTING OUT THE FIRE OF GOSSIP

I have just seen news footage of terrible bush fires in Australia. A drought followed by strong winds have created dangerous conditions threatening destruction and death. Once a fire has been started in that climate, it seems there's no stopping it.

Similarly, gossip spreads and scars like wildfire.[1]

We've thought about the destruction that gossip brings and we've considered the perfect conditions that enable gossip to rip through communities. Gossip spreads so quickly because we find it so delicious to hear. When hearts do not fear the Lord but are addicted to all manner of other things, gossip races through society causing destruction and death.

These dangerous conditions for gossip have been present since the Fall, but now, in the 21st century, we have a fuel for gossip that is like pouring paraffin on a fire – I'm thinking of the internet and, very specifically, social media. A post can be shared around the world in minutes. With social media at our fingertips, the speed that gossip can travel means that one post can bring carnage in seconds. So arguably we, more than any generation before us, need to know how to curb the destructive impact of gossip. Lives are being wrecked irreversibly because of it. How do we stop it?

> Without wood a fire goes out;
> without a gossip a quarrel dies down.
> *(Proverbs 26:20)*

My family used to live in a house with a log burner. The fire in the log burner roared and produced enough heat for the whole house (it was only a small house!), but the fire went out very quickly if we didn't keep stoking it with logs. The same is true with quarrels and gossip. Stop gossiping and the fire of rumour goes nowhere. So the answer is very simple: we can stop gossip in its tracks by not listening to it and not passing it on. Refusing to listen to gossip, or to speak or post it, is like refusing to put more logs in the log burner. If we create a culture in our churches where there is a blanket refusal to either listen to or pass on gossip, the fire of gossip would go out instantly. Everyone collectively refusing to pay any attention to gossip is as effective as pouring gallons of cold water on a tiny fire.

We can stop gossip by following these four steps :

1. Don't listen to gossip

A wicked person listens to deceitful lips;
a liar pays attention to a destructive tongue.
(Proverbs 17:4)

This proverb tells us that even listening to gossip ('deceitful lips' or 'a destructive tongue') is the action of a wicked person.

We've already seen in the previous chapter that:

To fear the LORD is to hate evil;
I hate pride and arrogance,
evil behaviour and perverse speech.
(Proverbs 8:13)

In other words, perverse speech is evil. Proverbs 17:4 adds that deceitful lips and destructive tongues are evil. Gossip is always deceitful or destructive or both. Gossip is deceitful when the whole truth is not told or the context is not fully given. Gossip is destructive when the whole truth *is* told but the motive is not pure – for example, when truthful information is passed on with the desire to hurt or damage the reputation of another person. Gossip is also destructive when the information passed on should have been kept confidential.

To put it another way, in Proverbs 17:4 Lady Wisdom tells us that even listening to gossip is the action of a wicked person. This is very challenging. Simply allowing ourselves to listen to gossip is to tolerate evil. Indeed, the very act of listening to (being one who 'pays attention to') gossip is lying. How shocking is that?

Of course, this begs the question of how am I lying when I simply listen to gossip? The answer is that we lie to ourselves when we convince ourselves that merely listening to gossip does not mean we're involved in gossiping. As we've already considered, if no-one listened to gossip, gossip would end. Therefore the very act of listening to gossip makes us complicit. By listening to a person's gossip, we give them even more appetite for their slanderous mission. When we pay attention to a gossiper, they are spurred on in the belief that others will also be a captive audience.

If that sounds a bit extreme to you, just consider the alternative. Imagine someone approaches you after church and begins telling you something about someone else in the church. Rather than just standing there and listening to it, you gently interrupt and say, 'I don't think it's appropriate for you to be telling me this. May I suggest that you speak to the person in question and not speak to anyone else about it?' Do you not think that will burst the bubble of the gossiper? And if they kept receiving that same response from everyone they spoke to, they'd soon give up their scandalous mischief. Refusing to listen to gossip is like pouring a bucket of cold water on the fire of gossip.

When it comes to social media, it will be a little harder to stop gossip in its tracks, but it's arguably even more important that we do. If we see a post that is spreading rumour (or worse), then a private message to the person who posted the information will at least make them realise that not everyone is gobbling down their juicy, libellous words. It may make them think twice about posting gossip in the future. Who knows, your carefully worded private text might even persuade them to delete the offending post from their newsfeed.

Raymond Ortlund is very helpful and extremely challenging here.

With Proverbs 31:8–9[2] in his sights, he writes:

> Do you speak up when others are put down? Or do you just stand there and listen in sinful silence as the blast of gossip and slander hits you in the face? God says, 'Open your mouth.' With every unkind word that goes unconfronted, a reputation dies.[3]

So, we're to stop listening to gossip and challenge it when we hear it. But we can take further action to minimise the chances of us even hearing gossip in the first place – and that's to avoid people who are gossips:

> A gossip betrays a confidence;
> so avoid anyone who talks too much.
>
> *(Proverbs 20:19)*

As we've already seen, Lady Wisdom actually tells us to avoid certain people. Once we realise that someone is a gossiper, we would do well not to spend time with them. Not for one moment do I think that this is telling us to have absolutely nothing to do with anyone who has ever gossiped – that would make us all very lonely people! Neither do I think that this is saying that we should cancel anyone who is a serial gossiper. I think the wisdom of this proverb is that we be wary of people who are gossips. If I know that someone can't keep confidences, I'd be wise to avoid sharing deep, personal or confidential issues with them. If I know that someone likes to gossip, I should be on my guard when I'm in conversation with them, knowing that they are likely to tell me things I shouldn't listen to.

As we consider how we might avoid those who gossip, let me ask you to be honest with yourself: are you someone who quite likes hearing the latest gossip? Do you seek out gossipers? Do you allow gossipers to get alongside you? Do you positively give time to gossipers because deep down you want to hear what they have to say? Proverbs 20:19 highlights the importance of avoiding situations where a gossiper can whisper their delicious secrets into my ear. I can, and should, avoid those situations.

This proverb also tells us that it's not wise to allow those who gossip to be in a role where they are party to information that should stay confidential. Therefore, gossipers should not be encouraged to be elders or permitted to sit on church councils.

So the first way to stop gossip is by not listening to it. A second step is not to talk too much.

2. Don't talk too much

Look again at Proverbs 20:19:

> A gossip betrays a confidence;
> so avoid anyone who talks too much.

This is a real challenge to me. Although I am very self-controlled when it comes to ensuring that I do not break confidences, I know that in some situations I can talk too much. I guess the law of averages says that the more I speak, the more chance there is that I'll let something slip. That is why there are a number of proverbs that counsel us not to talk too much, one of which is:

> When words are many, transgression is not lacking,
> but whoever restrains his lips is prudent.
> *(Proverbs 10:19,* ESV*)*

Lady Wisdom tells us speaking less is a great way to reduce the sins of the mouth. The more we talk, the greater the opportunity of sin being increased – and that includes the increased chance of gossip being multiplied. So, be prudent and hold your tongue[4] – and, if it were a thing, hold your keyboard. Post less. We would do well to stop and think before speaking or posting. How many of us open our mouths with our brain in neutral? When we speak without thinking, we may not be guilty of gossip through intent – we may genuinely not have intentionally spoken gossipy words – but we can still easily say things that harm others. Simply speaking less and typing less should reduce the amount of gossip spoken and confidences broken.

This popped up on my Facebook feed: 'The ability to speak several languages is an asset, but the ability to keep your mouth shut in any language is priceless.' It is helpful wisdom.

However, just speaking less is too minimalist. As followers of Christ, we don't want to settle for just avoiding gossip; we can do much better than that. Let's face it: we can speak less and still gossip. So Lady Wisdom tells us not only to speak less but to speak well.

3. Do speak well

Just consider these three proverbs from chapter 10:

> The mouth of the righteous is a fountain of life…
> *(Proverbs 10:11)*

> The lips of the righteous nourish many…
> *(Proverbs 10:21)*

> From the mouth of the righteous comes the
> fruit of wisdom…
> *(Proverbs 10:31)*

Those who fear the Lord are righteous people, and these three glorious proverbs tell us what should come out of the mouths of the righteous:

- Out of our mouths should gush words of life (verse 11).
- The things that leave our lips should nourish people (verse 21).
- Our words should be the delicious and nutritious fruit of wisdom (verse 31).

What a wonderful way to use our tongues! What a positive difference we could make every day of our lives if every time we did speak, we said things that build up, strengthen and point people in the way of life. I work with someone who does just this. Very naturally, they speak of the positive things they've been learning from the Bible. As a result, I invariably find myself feeling encouraged and spurred on to live for the Lord throughout the day. Please Lord may that be true of me, and may it be the case in your life too.

So far in this chapter, we've seen that we can snuff out the fires of gossip by not listening to gossip, by speaking less and by speaking well. Fourth, we can stop gossip by becoming a trustworthy, truthful person.

4. Do be a trustworthy person

Through the blessing of the upright a city is exalted,
but by the mouth of the wicked it is destroyed.
Whoever derides their neighbour has no sense,
but the one who has understanding
holds their tongue.
A gossip betrays a confidence,
but a trustworthy person keeps a secret.
(Proverbs 11:11–13)

Can you keep a secret? Those five words are often the enticing prelude to a gossip, which will lure you into listening to delicious but destructive words. But I'm not doing that here. I'm simply asking you that question of yourself. *Can* you keep a secret? Are you able to keep confidences?

Imagine a person who has struggled for years with a besetting sin. He bravely and honestly shares his struggle with a handful of people. But, desperately, one of that group of 'trusted' friends proves untrustworthy. Now it seems that the entire church knows everything about him – warts and all. Understandably, he finds it very hard to go to church. A brother has been ruined by one person being unable to keep a confidence.

We need to be people who can keep a secret. Gossips betray confidences, but trustworthy people keep secrets. So again, are you a trustworthy person? Can you hold your tongue? If your answer is 'No', then remember

Proverbs 11: 11: your wicked mouth could destroy a city. We need to have self-control (a fruit of the Spirit) in order to be trustworthy people who can keep our mouths shut.[5]

Gossip is like wildfire – it causes devastating destruction and even death. But we can take steps *not* to add fuel to the fire of gossip. We can act in ways that douse down the flames and snuff it out altogether. Don't listen to gossip. Don't talk too much. Instead, speak words that build up others and point them to the way of life. Be a trustworthy person. In short, be godly – be like Jesus.

14

WHEN WE DO GOSSIP

Alexander Pope famously penned, 'To err is human, to forgive divine.'[1] Long before Pope, the Bible taught this. Human beings are fallen and will sin, and one of the sins we will commit is gossiping. That's why it's been such a surprise to me that in 30 years of pastoral ministry, no-one has ever come to me to confess the sin of gossip. We do gossip. My prayer in writing this study through the book of Proverbs is that we might be so profoundly affected that we'll want to rid gossip from our lives and our fellowships. But even if we have this deep heartfelt desire, we will commit the sin of gossip in the days, weeks, months and years that lie ahead. So in this chapter I want to consider what we do when we fail.

For some, reading this book has been deeply convicting. Thank you for sticking with it. The conviction you are under is weighing heavily on you. You have been convicted that you are a serial gossiper and that your gossiping has caused considerable pain and hurt to others. But if this book has had that effect on you, then be encouraged. Yes, you heard me correctly, be encouraged – because the Holy Spirit is doing His work in you through His Word. Be encouraged and do not feel condemned.[2] The wonder of the gospel is that forgiveness in Christ is always available for repentant sinners.

In a moment we'll think more about the wonderful gospel of grace and forgiveness, but before we do, consider these comforting words of assurance:

> My son, do not despise the LORD's discipline,
> and do not resent his rebuke,
> because the LORD disciplines those he loves,
> as a father the son he delights in.
> *(Proverbs 3:11–12)*

A strong feeling of conviction and rebuke is a sign that you are a child of our Heavenly Father.

Many years ago, at a Christianity Explored course I was leading, I met a young man in his mid-twenties. I'll call him Geoff. On week one, he told the group that he wasn't even sure why he was there and that he certainly didn't believe that there was a God. At the end of week two, he was different – he was quietly reflecting on all that he had heard. At the start of week three, he declared to the group that he'd become a Christian. The joy on his face was something to behold. It was a remarkable turnaround.

On week four, he looked very downhearted and didn't say a word all evening. At the end of the meeting, as everyone else drifted off, I asked Geoff how he was. 'I've blown it,' he said. He explained that he'd been on a business trip to Amsterdam for a couple of days and on the first evening he went out with his colleagues. In his words, he 'got absolutely slaughtered'. He'd got so drunk that in the morning he could barely remember anything about the night before. He felt, 'I've completely let Jesus down.' He was deeply convicted of his sin.

I asked him if he'd ever got drunk before (though I was pretty sure I knew the answer). 'Of course I have,' he said. 'Every time I go away on work trips, my colleagues and I spend the evenings getting as drunk as skunks.'

'And, in the past, when you've drunk like that, how have you felt about it?' I asked.

Geoff said, 'Apart from the pounding headache in the morning, I've never really given it another thought.'

So I asked Geoff, 'Do you see the change?' I continued, 'Of course, it's not good that you got drunk last week. But you've been drunk many times before, and you've never given it a second thought. This time, you feel dreadful – and not just because of the hangover! That is the work of God in you.'

In the weeks that followed, Geoff and I talked together about taking steps not to get drunk again. In that moment, though, Geoff could see that his deep conviction was a mark that the Holy Spirit was working in him, and that His loving Heavenly Father was graciously disciplining him. Geoff understood His Heavenly Father's rebuke as a mark of His love for him.

Similarly, feeling conviction about your gossiping is a sign that God loves you as His child.

I had wonderful parents – sadly, they're both dead now. Mum and Dad loved me and my brother unconditionally and provided everything we needed. When we were growing up, Mum and Dad didn't have much, but we never went without. They encouraged us and did their best to help us take the opportunities before us. I'm grateful for my parents. They gave us such a terrific start in life – and that included discipline. As I look back, I can't think of one occasion when I was pleased to be rebuked. On the many occasions when they disciplined me (and it was many because I was often naughty!), I didn't once say to Mum and Dad, 'Thank you for grounding me – that is so loving and kind of you!' But I am so grateful that they loved me enough to correct me. Being a parent myself, I see clearly now that my parents' discipline was a mark of their love for me.

Some of you won't have had the privilege of growing up with good parents. You may have grown up under the tyranny of a father who was too harsh – and that may well have damaged you. Others may have had to cope with an absent dad. Some may have been raised by a weak father – someone who never disciplined you. Having to cope with an overbearing father is very different from having an absent father or a weak dad. But please know that while it is wrong and extremely unhelpful to have a harsh father, it is equally wrong and extremely unhelpful to never be disciplined by your father. Neither is good. We learn so much through discipline. Being disciplined correctly should prevent us from making monumental mistakes in the future. Appropriate, propionate discipline – in a context of oodles of unconditional loving encouragement – is very good for us. It will help us, providing we do not despise discipline.

As you feel the weight of conviction for your gossiping, please know that this is the discipline of your perfect loving Heavenly Father – He's disciplining you because He loves you. He wants to rescue you from the path that leads to death. His correction may be weighing very heavily right now, but your Heavenly Father is never too harsh. Neither is He weak, and He won't be absent. He loves you too much to leave you making mistakes and walking down a road to destruction. So, 'do not despise the LORD's discipline, and do not resent his rebuke' (Proverbs 3:11).

The book of Proverbs speaks often of the danger of despising discipline,[3] but we'll just look at a couple here. First:

> Those who disregard discipline despise themselves,
> but the one who heeds correction
> gains understanding.
> *(Proverbs 15:32)*

This proverb is very striking – ignoring discipline is self-hatred, or self-harm. The Lord disciplines us to turn us from death and towards life. If we disregard His discipline, we are self-harming as we continue to walk along a road of destruction.

But, second, if we take note of the Lord's rebuke, we'll find that:

> ...correction and instruction
> are the way to life.
> *(Proverbs 6:23)*

How kind of our Heavenly Father to correct, rebuke and discipline us. It puts us on the road to life.

Before we move on to the forgiveness that the Lord wants us to know, let me encourage you to remember how ghastly and uncomfortable the heavy hand of the Lord feels.[4] Being able to remember that deeply uncomfortable feeling is a kindness of God. The deep conviction of the Holy Spirit weighing heavily on us is part of the way lasting change comes into our lives. Whenever the Lord has brought my own sinful failures to light, I have never enjoyed it at the time (and rarely welcome it). However, the Lord has used my heart-wrenching and deeply uncomfortable conviction of sin to give me the desire to never go that way again.

With that deep conviction from God about your own gossiping, you must then run. Run into the arms of God. Run towards the one who loves you and wants you and has all the resources to forgive you. You'll be tempted to run away from Him – perhaps you feel ashamed and don't want to talk to your Heavenly Father. But genuine fear of the Lord always see us running *to* Him.

When my twin daughters were toddlers, they used to love playing a game called 'Lions'. The game was very straightforward. Susannah and Bethan would go into another room in the house; I would get on all fours, crawl into that room and roar like a lion. They would then run past me into a different room; I would next crawl into that room, roaring again like a lion. The girls would giggle and scream with delight, and as the game went on, they would whip themselves into an excitable frenzy. 'Louder, Daddy, louder,' they would shout, wanting me to produce a bigger and bigger 'roar' as I entered the room.

On one occasion – when the girls' giggling had turned into uncontrollable laughter and their pleas of 'louder' had become ever more desperate – I got up off my hands and knees, stood up and ran into the next room, letting out the biggest roar I could muster. The girls burst into tears ... and ran towards me, grabbing hold of my legs.

Once Mummy had arrived to sort out the 'mess' I'd created, and the girls had calmed down, I realised the girls' reaction was a brilliant illustration of what it means to fear the Lord. My girls were genuinely frightened of me as I roared like a lion. They couldn't escape me. I was bigger than them and more powerful than them. But I was also their daddy. In their fear, they instinctively knew that the safest thing to do was to run to me.[5]

To fear the Lord will result in us running to the Lord. Yes, our sin is serious – very serious. Yes, God is not to be trifled with – He is Almighty God and Lord of all. But He is the 'LORD' – the covenant-keeping, gracious, merciful, compassionate, loving and forgiving Father God.[6]

> Through love and faithfulness sin is atoned for;
> through the fear of the LORD evil is avoided.
> *(Proverbs 16:6)*

Through God's love and faithfulness – faithfulness to His promises and to Himself – He has atoned for sin. Jesus – the sinless Saviour, the one who never gossiped – took the punishment for your sin and mine as He died on the cross. His atoning sacrifice is enough to cover every sin, and that includes every sin of the mouth. At the cross Jesus paid the punishment for *every* occasion we have spoken badly, wrongly, hurtfully, callously and vindictively. Every word of jealousy and revenge that has left our lips has been paid for at the cross. Every word that has come out of our mouths from a heart that desired power and control has been cancelled at Calvary. Jesus died for every time you've gossiped and for every reason you gossiped. You can be forgiven as you run to your Heavenly Father in repentance and faith. His forgiveness is free – totally free – but it isn't cheap. It cost Jesus His life. That's quite a thought. Jesus died for gossip. That's how bad gossip is.

So feel your sin, run to Him and then remember what it cost Jesus for you to be forgiven for your gossiping and the hurt it's caused. That should leave you with a sense of awe and wonder and fear of the Lord – and that is what changes people and ensures 'evil is avoided'.

Then soak up this proverb:

> If you turn at my reproof,
> behold, I will pour out my spirit to you;
>   I will make my words known to you.
> *(Proverbs 1:23, ESV)*

To 'turn' here is a word of repentance. It's a decisive word. In the context of the book of Proverbs, it's us saying, 'I want to be wise. I want to fear the Lord.' This is so much more than simply trying harder, which never works for long. As we were considering in chapter 11, it is a fear of the Lord that brings about lasting change. Excitingly, the proverb above tells us that as we respond to the Lord's reproof in repentance, we will come to know Him better and fear Him all the more. Repentance ('If you turn at my reproof') is immediately followed by the promise that the Holy Spirit (who is the author of the Bible) will open up God's Word to us: 'I will make my words known to you.' Decisive repentance results in new insight as we read the Bible. As God's Word comes more alive to us, we'll have an even greater desire to live as we should in the fear of the Lord.

Running to the Lord in genuine repentance will result in us knowing Him more and, as a result, living more faithfully for Him in the days ahead.

15

GOING FORWARD – A DESIRE TO END GOSSIP

Having read this far, I'm hoping you're convinced that getting rid of gossip from our lives will be good for everyone. Banishing gossip will mean others aren't hurt, it will mean we don't walk down the road to destruction and it will please the Lord.

Ultimately this is a heart issue, but there are some helpful disciplines we can put in place in our lives. These will help us make constructive steps to eradicate gossip from our lives.

1. Study God's Word

Look at these two proverbs:

The fear of the LORD is a fountain of life,
    turning a person from the snares of death.
(Proverbs 14:27)

The teaching of the wise is a fountain of life,
    turning a person from the snares of death.
(Proverbs 13:14)

These two proverbs are almost identical – they both tell us how to avoid 'the snares of death'. But note how they differ. This difference is found in the first five words of each, telling us that we avoid the snares of death through:

'The fear of the LORD' (Proverbs 14:27), and
'The teaching of the wise' (Proverbs 13:14)

At one level these two proverbs teach us two different things we need in order to avoid the snares of death – namely to fear the Lord and to listen to the teaching of the wise. But if we engage with these two verses together, we see how each proverb sheds light on the other.

So when I read Proverbs 14:27, I should ask, 'What will it look like to fear the Lord and so avoid the snares of death?' The answer comes in Proverbs 13:14. Those who fear the Lord will listen to the teaching of the wise – that's how I avoid the snares of death. And it works the other way round too. Those who listen to the teaching of the wise will fear the Lord – and fearing the Lord will save me from the snares of death.

If you fear the Lord, you'll read and obey the Bible. If you read and obey the Bible, you'll fear the Lord.

This is a wonderful thought, not just for getting rid of gossip from our lives, but for growing in obedience in any area. Fear of the Lord is what will make me live as I should (as we saw in chapter 11). By fearing the Lord and studying His Word, I'll love and fear Him more, and this will motivate me to live obediently to His ways.

This means that if you want to get rid of gossip, you will search hard for the teaching of the wise. This is found in the Bible – not just in Proverbs, but on every page of God's Word. So be sure to be involved in a church where the Bible is taught well and faithfully. When the Bible is taught, on a Sunday or at a midweek Bible study, be all ears. Be attentive. Be alert. And study the Bible yourself each day. If you're not sure where to start, get some good Bible study notes, or find some good commentaries to read alongside your daily Bible reading.

Perhaps this sounds like a lot of effort? However, the book of Proverbs tells us to be people who search for wisdom with more effort than we give to earning money and increasing our wealth. Lady Wisdom tells us to search for wisdom as if it were buried treasure:

> My son, if you accept my words
>   and store up my commands within you,
> turning your ear to wisdom
>   and applying your heart to understanding –indeed,
> if you call out for insight

and cry aloud for understanding,and if you look for it as for silver
and search for it as for hidden treasure,then you will understand the fear of the LORD
and find the knowledge of God.
(Proverbs 2:1–5)

Choose my instruction instead of silver,
knowledge rather than choice gold,
for wisdom is more precious than rubies,
and nothing you desire can compare with her.
(Proverbs 8:10–11)

Having a desire for wisdom and a longing to fear the Lord needs to lead to an investment in studying God's Word. It requires finding a good Bible-teaching church, making it a priority to attend on Sundays, going regularly to a midweek Bible study and spending good quality time each day in God's Word.

2. Love God's Word

But I need to do more than just study God's Word. If I'm going to live an obedient Christian life, I need to grow in my love for God's Word.

Eat honey, my son, for it is good;
honey from the comb is sweet to your taste.
Know also that wisdom is like honey for you:

> If you find it, there is a future hope for you,
> and your hope will not be cut off.
>
> *(Proverbs 24:13–14)*

This is a delicious proverb, not least of all as it completely reverses the way many of us think when it comes to obeying the Lord and getting to know His Word. I think it's fair to say that many of us, much of the time – and all of us, at least some of the time – consider obedience to the Lord to be a bit like swallowing bitter-tasting medicine. We'll take our daily dose because we're convinced it will do us good, but we don't enjoy the experience. The picture painted in Proverbs 24:13–14 could not be more different.

Wisdom is like honey. It is sweet. Ray Ortlund brilliantly suggests that this proverb tells us to go and cook a pancake, put some butter on it, watch it melt, then pour honey over it. As we take a mouthful and experience the wonderful sweetness of the honey, we are to know wisdom is like that for our soul.[1] Wisdom is sweet. Receiving wisdom from the Lord is very, very good for you. Living wisdom is deeply satisfying. Knowing wisdom and then living it out is a treat for your soul – like honey to the lips.

It reminds me of Jesus' words: 'I have come that they may have life, and have it to the full' (John 10:10). Living for Jesus is not just something I ought to do, and is not just essential in order to be saved from hell. Living for Jesus is so much more enriching than that – living with Jesus is fabulous. Living His way is the sweetest way to live. If I believe this, I'll long to study God's Word, I'll long to gain wisdom and I'll long to live it out – not just because it will do me good, but because it *is* good.

So, be kind to yourself and care for your soul. Every day, treat yourself to a spiritual honey fest. Do all you can to get wisdom and live by it.

3. Obey God's Word

But studying God's Word and having a love of God's Word is still not enough. The Pharisees of Jesus' day did that! We need to be people who obey God's Word too, for it is in obeying the Word that our hearts are protected. Lady Wisdom says:

> Above all else, guard your heart,
> for everything you do flows from it.
> Keep your mouth free of perversity;
> keep corrupt talk far from your lips.
> *(Proverbs 4:23–24)*

We guard our hearts by keeping corrupt talk from our lips. Every time you exercise self-control and restrain from gossip, you guard your heart. Every time you refuse to let bad things come out of your mouth, you are doing your heart a great favour. Not gossiping is good for you.

But there's more here. Yes, as we keep our mouths clean, our hearts are guarded and kept clean too;

additionally, keeping our hearts clean means our lives will be purer too:

> 'for everything you do flows from [your heart]'
> *(Proverbs 4:23).*

What a great way to live going forward.

- Studying God's Word will make you grow in your love for the Lord – which is good for you.
- Loving God's Word will give your soul a treat – which is good for you.
- Obeying God's Word will guard your heart – which is good for you.
- And doing all this, you'll live as you should – which is good for everyone.

Why would we *not* want to live like this?

16

A GOSSIP-FREE LIFE

Can you picture a gossip free-life?

A life where no-one is hurt by gossip. Where no-one experiences the deep pain of feeling they've been betrayed by friends.

A life where you never have to wonder what is said about you when you leave the room. Where no-one speaks out of turn behind your back.

A life where rumour isn't spread on the internet. Where nothing scandalous is put on social media.

A life where reputations aren't wrecked by loose tongues. Where no-one is lying awake at night turning over the agony of their lives being ruined by the scandalous comments of others.

A life where you can be sure that your confidences will be kept. Where it's safe to be vulnerable with others and to tell them deep and personal things.

A life where the information shared with you in conversation is always fitting. Where you never have to wonder if it's appropriate to listen to what is being said to you.

A life where lives aren't destroyed and ended by scurrilous people seeking revenge or jealously attempting to put someone down in order to raise themselves up.

Such a gossip-free life sounds wonderful. It's a life we can look forward to in the eternal heavenly new creation. I can't wait.

But it's also a life that has been lived perfectly here on earth – once. Look at Jesus. Never did He speak words that were inappropriate. Not once did He speak from a selfish motive. Jesus did not pass on the personal information of others in order to persuade people to follow Him. In short, Jesus didn't gossip. The Bible tells us that He was 'tempted in every way, just as we are – yet he did not sin' (Hebrews 4:15). Therefore, Jesus would have felt the powerful temptation to speak badly of others in order to protect His own reputation. Jesus would have felt the tantalising desire to just stand there and listen to gossip without stopping the gossiper in their tracks. But Jesus never succumbed to any of those temptations.

I know we'll never be perfectly like Jesus this side of glory, but from the moment we are converted, our Father wants us to be conformed more and more into the likeness of His Son.[1] Seeking to rid ourselves, and our fellowships, of the destructive sin of gossip is something God wants for us. Therefore we can be sure He will help us in the battle to eradicate gossip from our lives. He wants us to be a gossip-free people.

Could our churches be like that? It needs to start with us.

NOTES

Introduction: The confession I've never heard

1 Jerry Bridges, *Respectable Sins* (Tyndall House Publishers, 2017).

1. Gossip is tasty

1 'What does the Bible say about gossip?', gotquestions.org: www.gotquestions.org/gossip-Bible.html

2. Gossip destroys

1 https://www.mentalfloss.com/article/72892/9-false-rumors-real-life-consequences

4. Gossip will kill you!

1 Raymond C. Ortlund Jr, *Proverbs: Wisdom that Works* (Crossway, 2012), p. 31.

2 For a biblical understanding of what it means to 'fear the Lord', see Michael Reeves' excellent work, *Rejoice and Tremble* (Crossway, 2021).

3 If you want to study the entire book of Proverbs, you will do no better than to get hold of a copy of Raymond C. Ortlund Jr, *Proverbs: Wisdom that Works*.

4 This sounds a lot like Jesus' words in the sermon of the mount. He taught that we can walk down one of two roads: one that leads to life; the other leading to destruction (Matthew 7:13–14).

5 1 Corinthians 6:9–11 makes it clear that Christians have left behind a life of persistent sexual immorality.

6 Jeff Robinson, 'What's Wrong with Gossip?' (The Gospel Coalition blog, January 2022).

5. Gossip is addictive

1 Ricky Naputi was the focus of the Channel 5 documentary *The Man Who Ate Himself to Death* and the American TV network TLC followed him for their documentary *900 Pound Man: The Race against Time*.

2 Of course we are all addicted to food, but Ricky Naputi was addicted to the wrong kinds of food and ate too much food, and so it killed him.

6. The addiction of friendship

1 I have changed the names and circumstances of all the people I mention in this book so that no-one can be identified. It would be ironic if I could be accused of gossiping through the writing of this book!

2 See chapter 2 of Vaughan Roberts, *True Friendship* (10Publishing, 2013).

7. The addiction of power and control

1 Manfred Kets de Vries explains how this is the case: 'The pursuit of power may also have a neurochemical component. Having power over others has an intoxicating effect. It boosts testosterone, which in turn increases the supply of dopamine (a feel-good neurotransmitter) in the brain's reward system. This dopamine rush explains the addictive quality of power and why it's so hard to let it go.

'However, an excess of dopamine can impact cognitive and emotional functioning. It can reduce empathy, promote hubristic and impulsive behaviour, thus contributing to gross errors of judgment and unnecessary risk taking. Eventually, people with too much power may even lose their sense of reality and their moral bearings. Before they know it, they live in an echo chamber, believing their own press and imagining that they are infallible.' See Manfred Kets de Vries, 'Are you addicted to power?' in *Management Issues* (9 May 2018).

2 We see exactly how often Solomon addresses his son(s) in these verses: Proverbs 1:8, 10, 15; 2:1; 3:1, 11, 21; 4:1, 20; 5:1; 6:1, 20; 7:1.

3 We are told this fact in 1 Kings 4:30.

8. The addiction of revenge

1 I don't think Swift is using the word 'karma' here as it would be technically defined by Hinduism or Buddhism. Rather, she is using it in the colloquial way: that when somebody does something good, good will come their

way, whereas bad things happen because we've done something bad to someone else. In short, you get what you deserve.

9. The addiction of jealousy

1 See Paul E. Mullen, 'Jealousy and Violence', *Hong Kong Journal of Psychiatry*, vol. 5 (1995), pp. 18–24.

2 Raymond C. Ortlund Jr, *Proverbs: Wisdom that Works*, p. 162.

3 *The J. I. Packer Classic Collection*, compiled by Thomas Womack (NavPress, 2010), p. 57.

4 I first came across the idea of our inner lawyer from the Christian speaker and author Paul Tripp.

10. Pause for thought

1 If you want to consider self-control in more detail, you might consider my book *Willing but Weak: Fighting to Put Self-Control at the Heart of Christian Discipleship* (10Publishing, 2020).

2 I commend to you Tim Chester's book *You Can Change* (IVP, 2008) to help you address heart issues and work through how you can change.

12. The heart of the matter

1 Michael Reeves, *Rejoice and Tremble*, p. 138.

2 Michael Reeves, *Rejoice and Tremble*, p. 138.

13. Putting out the fire of gossip

1 Precisely this imagery is used for the sins of the tongue in James 3:5–6: 'Likewise, the tongue is a small part of the body, but it makes great boasts. Consider what a great forest is set on fire by a small spark. The tongue also is a fire, a world of evil among the parts of the body. It corrupts the whole body, sets the whole course of one's life on fire, and is itself set on fire by hell.'

2 Proverbs 31:8–9 says, 'Speak up for those who cannot speak for themselves, for the rights of all who are destitute. Speak up and judge fairly; defend the rights of the poor and needy.'

3 Raymond C. Ortlund Jr, *Proverbs: Wisdom that Works*, p. 134.

4 See also Proverbs 11:12.

5 For a study of self-control, see my book *Willing but Weak*.

14. When we do gossip

1 This quote comes from Alexander Pope's 1711 treatise, *An Essay on Criticism*.

2 Remember Romans 8:1: 'Therefore, there is now no condemnation for those who are in Christ Jesus.'

3 See Proverbs 10:17; 12:1; 13:18; 15:5, 32; 19:20

4 See Psalm 32:4.

5 This illustration was first published in my book *Intentional* (10Publishing, 2016).

6 See Exodus 34:6–7.

15. Going forward – a desire to end gossip

1 Raymond C. Ortlund Jr, Proverbs: Wisdom that Works, p. 186.

16. A gossip-free life

2 See Romans 8:29.